PIANO • VOCAL SELECTIONS

Once Upon A Mattress

Music by
MARY RODGERS

Lyrics by
MARSHALL BARER

Book by
DEAN FULLER **JAY THOMPSON** **MARSHALL BARER**

4 **Shy**

8 **Sensitivity**

12 **Very Soft Shoes**

17 **In a Little While**

20 **Happily Ever After**

24 **Yesterday I Loved You**

28 **Normandy**

Artwork by Frank "Fraver" Verlizzo for R&H Theatricals

ISBN 978-0-88188-101-1

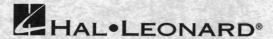

Visit Hal Leonard Online at
www.halleonard.com

Contact us:
Hal Leonard
7777 West Bluemound Road
Milwaukee, WI 53213
Email: info@halleonard.com

In Europe, contact:
Hal Leonard Europe Limited
42 Wigmore Street
Marylebone, London, W1U 2RN
Email: info@halleonardeurope.com

In Australia, contact:
Hal Leonard Australia Pty. Ltd.
4 Lentara Court
Cheltenham, Victoria, 3192 Australia
Email: info@halleonard.com.au

once upon a mattress

Produced by T. EDWARD HAMBLETON, NORRIS HOUGHTON & WILLIAM and JEAN ECKART
First performance May 11, 1959 at the Phoenix Theatre, New York

Directed by GEORGE ABBOTT

Dances and Musical Numbers Staged by Joe Layton
Scenery and Costumes by William and Jean Eckart
Lighting by Tharon Musser
Musical Direction by Hal Hastings
Orchestrations by Hershy Kay, Arthur Beck and Carroll Huxley
Dance Music Arranged by Roger Adams

Cast of Characters
(In order of appearance)

Prologue

MINSTREL	Harry Snow
PRINCE	Jim Maher
PRINCESS	Chris Karner
QUEEN	Gloria Stevens

WIZARD	Robert Weil
PRINCESS NUMBER TWELVE	Mary Stanton
LADY ROWENA	Dorothy Aull
LADY MERRILL	Patsi King
PRINCE DAUNTLESS	Joe Bova
THE QUEEN	Jane White
LADY LUCILLE	Luce Ennis
LADY LARKEN	Anne Jones
SIR STUDLEY	Jerry Newby
THE KING	Jack Gilford
JESTER	Matt Mattox
SIR HARRY	Allen Case
PRINCESS WINNIFRED	Carol Burnett
SIR HAROLD	David Neuman
LADY BEATRICE	Gloria Stevens
SIR LUCE	Tom Mixon
LADY MABELLE	Chris Karner
THE NIGHTINGALE OF SAMARKAND	Ginny Perlowin
LADY DOROTHY	Dorothy D'Honau
SIR CHRISTOPHER	Christopher Edwards
LORD HOWARD	Howard Parker
LADY DORA	Dorothy Frank
SIR DANIEL	Dan Resin
SIR STEVEN	Jim Stevenson
LORD PATRICK	Julian Patrick

SHY

Words by MARSHALL BARER
Music by MARY RODGERS

SENSITIVITY

Words by MARSHALL BARER
Music by MARY RODGERS

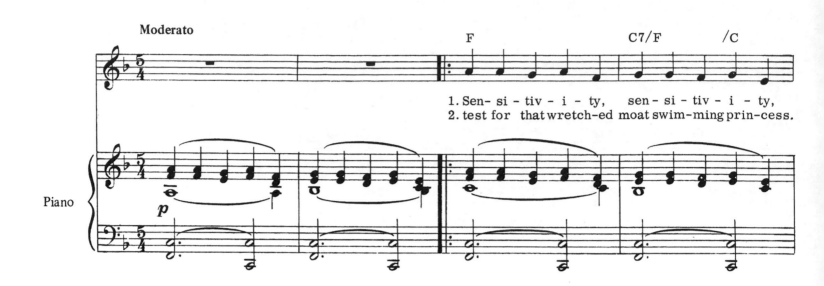

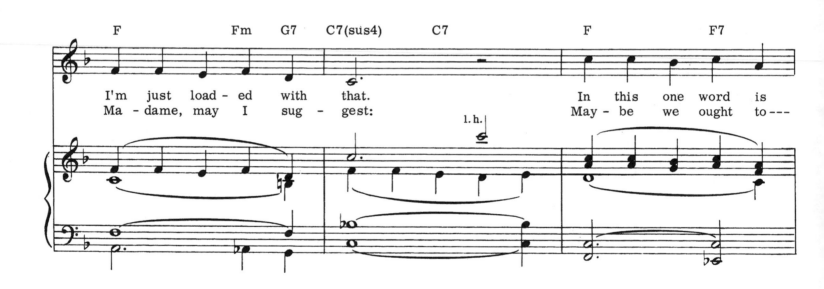

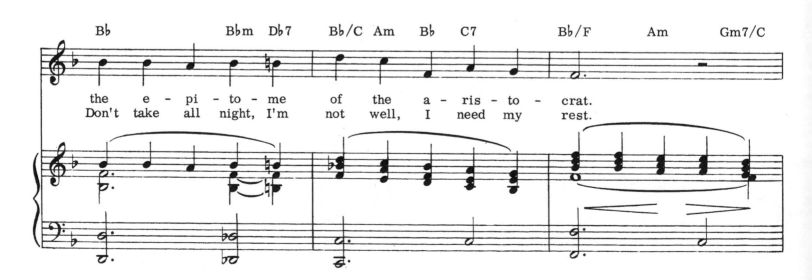

VERY SOFT SHOES

Words by MARSHALL BARER
Music by MARY RODGERS

I am far from sen - ti - men - tal or ro - man - tic.

And I like to think I'm strict - ly up to date. But at

times the danc - ing gets a bit too fran - tic In these

hec - tic days of four - teen twen - ty eight. So, in - dulge me if I

IN A LITTLE WHILE

Words by MARSHALL BARER
Music by MARY RODGERS

HAPPILY EVER AFTER

Words by MARSHALL BARER
Music by MARY RODGERS

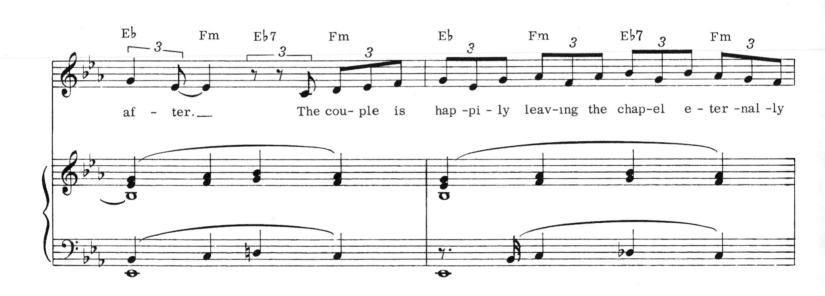

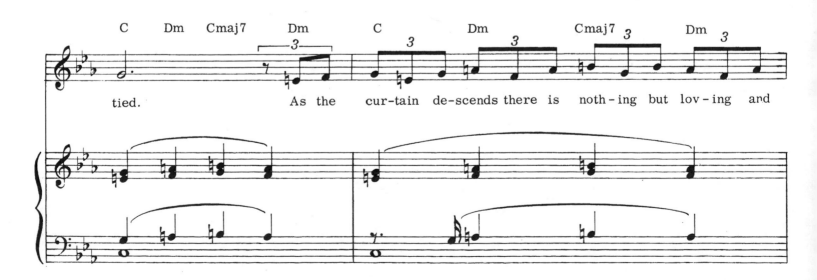

laugh-ter. When the fair-y tale ends, the her-o-ine's al-ways a bride.

El - la, the girl of the cin - ders,_ Did the wash and the walls and the win - ders,_ But she
white was so pret-ty, they tell us____ That the queen was in - sult - ed and jeal -ous__ When the

land - ed a prince who was brawn-y and blue-eyed and blond.
mir - ror de - clared that Snow White was the fair - est of all.

Still I hon - est - ly doubt that___ she could ev - er have done it with-out that___ Cra - zy
She was dumped on the bor - der___ but was saved by some men who a-dored her.___ Oh, I

YESTERDAY I LOVED YOU

Words by MARSHALL BARER
Music by MARY RODGERS

NORMANDY

Words by MARSHALL BARER
Music by MARY RODGERS

hap-pen when an A-pril day is done. ____

There's a mo-ment af-ter the sun-set when the

sky goes sud-den-ly green; And the world stands hushed and

wait-ing for the first white stars to con-vene. When you